GENTLE

and

LOWLY

Study Guide

Dane Ortlund

CROSSWAY®

WHEATON, ILLINOIS

Gentle and Lowly Study Guide

Published by Crossway

1300 Crescent Street

Wheaton, Illinois 60187

Cover Design: Jordan Singer

Cover Image: Photo © Christie's Images / Bridgeman Images

First printing 2021

Printed in the United States of America

Trade paperback ISBN: 978-1-4335-8013-0

Crossway is a publishing ministry of Good News Publishers.

LSC 31 30 29 28 27 26 25 24 23 22
12 11 10 9 8 7 6 5 4 3 2

CONTENTS

INTRODUCTION

"Great truths are not meant to be hurriedly absorbed or quickly downloaded. They are meant to be slowly digested. Pondered slowly, reflectively, and thereby taken way down deep into our hearts to stay."

DANE ORTLUND

The *Gentle and Lowly Study Guide* is designed to enhance your reflective reading and understanding of Dane Ortlund's *Gentle and Lowly: The Heart of Christ for Sinners and Sufferers*. Through a number of questions, this guide leads you through small sections of the book, helping you ponder slowly Ortlund's insights on the heart of Christ that are drawn from Scripture and some of the church's greatest theologians. The hope is that this booklet will guide you through the book *Gentle and Lowly*, and, more importantly, into a deeper understanding of our gentle and lowly Lord and his heart for you: "Come to me, all who labor and are heavy laden, and I will give you rest. Take my yoke upon you, and learn from me, for I am gentle and lowly in heart, and you will find rest for your souls" (Matt. 11:28–29).

This study guide has been designed for use either in small-group discussion or in individual study. Leaders of small-group discussion will find the questions paced for multiple weeks of reflection and mutual growth. Those who use this study guide for individual study are nevertheless encouraged to find a discussion partner to work with together through this material. In doing so, appreciation for the deepest heart of Christ will intensify as one saint refreshes and sharpens another. May God grace you with his very presence as you pursue this study.

A NOTE ABOUT THE *GENTLE AND LOWLY VIDEO STUDY*

This study guide was designed to be used alongside the *Gentle and Lowly Video Study*, a companion 10-session video series featuring pastor Dane Ortlund.

Throughout this study guide, you will see prompts directing you to watch the corresponding teaching video. While these videos are not required in order to use this study guide effectively, they were specifically designed to reinforce the core message of the book while encouraging personal reflection and group discussion—leading readers to an ever deeper understanding of the heart of God for sinners and sufferers.

To learn more about the *Gentle and Lowly Video Study*, please visit crossway.org/gentleandlowlyvideo.

LESSON 1

I am gentle and lowly in heart.

MATTHEW 11:29

Chapters 1 & 2

Teaching Video 1

1. What role does the heart play in a person's life? What are the implications of this for what Jesus says about his own heart? (pp. 18–19)

2. What are some of the ways in which the New Testament depicts the "lowly"? What does this teach us about Jesus? (pp. 19–20)

3. What difference does it make in your everyday life that "no one in human history has ever been more approachable than Jesus Christ"? (p. 20)

4. What does Jesus mean when he says, "My yoke is easy"? What does he not mean? (p. 22)

5. According to Thomas Goodwin, what misconception is Jesus correcting when he describes himself as "gentle and lowly"? How do you find yourself falling prey to that misconception in your own thinking? (pp. 23–24)

6. How do Jesus's actions throughout the four Gospels manifest his heart for sinners? To whom does he naturally gravitate? (pp. 25–27)

7. Does stressing the compassionate love of Christ underemphasize other elements of his character? What considerations must we keep in mind as we answer this question? (pp. 28–29)

8. How is Jesus's natural impulse toward sin and suffering different from our typical instinct? What can we learn from his example? (p. 30)

9. How does Jesus reverse the interplay between the Old Testament categories of clean and unclean? What relevance does this have for your own life? (pp. 30–31)

10. How do we today receive and experience the same compassionate love that Christ demonstrated in his earthly ministry? (pp. 32–33)

LESSON 2

We do not have a high priest who is unable to sympathize with our weaknesses.

HEBREWS 4:15

Chapters 3–5

Teaching Video 2

1. Before approaching chapter 3, how would you have answered the question, What makes Jesus happy? Has this chapter changed your answer in any way? (pp. 35–38)

2. How would you put the quote from Thomas Goodwin on pages 37–38 into your own words? Is this the Christ you have been following and have instinctively believed to be there?

3. What was the joy awaiting Christ (Heb. 12:2)? (pp. 39–40)

4. Have you deeply considered Christ's "solidarity" with you in your Christian discipleship? What does this mean for your everyday life? (pp. 45–46)

5. Consider the way in which Jesus is described in the first two full paragraphs on page 47. Is this how you tend to think of Jesus, or do you tend to emphasize his deity and downplay his real humanity in your own thoughts of him?

6. It is natural for us to think that anguish and pain are an isolating reality in our life. But how does this chapter clarify things for us? (pp. 48–49)

7. What is the significance of the common Greek word root *dunamenon*, as underscored at the bottom of page 52?

8. Consider the word "gently" in Hebrews 5:2, speaking of the priests and of Jesus as the perfect priest. Does this word surprise you in any way? What is a difficulty in your life right now that this word calms and heals? (pp. 53–56)

9. Consider the image of a father that John Owen uses in the block quote on page 55. What is Owen saying about the depth of feeling that Christ experiences toward his sinning people?

10. What is the difference between fixing your attention on your sin versus fixing your attention on Christ? (p. 57)

LESSON 3

Whoever comes to me I will never cast out.

JOHN 6:37

Chapters 6 & 7

Teaching Video 3

1. What is a particularly precious truth to you emerging from the first half of John 6:37 ("All that the Father gives me will come to me")? (pp. 60–61)

2. In light of the John Bunyan quote on page 62, consider your own heart. What are some ways in which you find yourself wiggling out from under Christ's promise never to cast you out? What in your life renders it difficult to believe Christ will never cast you out?

3. Do you find your heart operating in a way akin to the mock dialogue between us and Jesus on pages 63–64? How does John 6:37 surprise you?

4. What do you believe to be ultimately determinative of your security in Christ's heart: your hold of him or his hold of you? What does Scripture teach? (pp. 64–65)

5. What does the author mean by "the perseverance of the heart of Christ"? What does this perseverance mean for your life this week? (pp. 65–66)

6. Why do we not feel the full weight and horror of our sin? (pp. 67–68)

7. What do Christ's holiness and purity mean for the way he feels about the sin of those who do not belong to him? What do his holiness and purity mean for the way he feels about the sin of those who do belong to him? (pp. 69–70)

8. How would you summarize in your own words what Thomas Goodwin is saying in the quote on pages 70–71?

9. In what way(s) does Hosea 11 surprise you about God and his holiness? (pp. 72–74)

10. As you conclude your reflecting on chapter 7, how has your view of divine holiness been changed or clarified?

LESSON 4

He always lives to make intercession for them.

HEBREWS 7:25

Chapters 8 & 9 | *Teaching Video 4*

1. Do you think much about what Jesus is doing right now? Has the reality of his intercession been a part of your regular reflection and discipleship? (p. 77)

2. What is the connection between Christ's intercession and Christ's heart? (pp. 78–79)

3. What does it mean that Jesus intercedes for us? How does that calm and reassure you right now? (pp. 79–81)

4. Reflect on the phrase "to the uttermost" in Hebrews 7:25. How is that phrase, translating a single Greek word (*panteles*), a comfort to you? (pp. 82–83)

5. Have you realized that, if you are in Christ, he himself is praying for you? How does this transform or strengthen your own prayer life? (p. 84)

6. What is the difference between an intercessor and an advocate? How does the notion of advocacy develop that of intercession? (p. 87)

7. What are some truths about Jesus the advocate, as taught in 1 John 2:1? (p. 89)

8. What is the slight difference between what we are told in Hebrews 7:25 and in 1 John 2:1? How does John Bunyan explain the difference? (p. 90)

9. Do you see in yourself the deep-seated impulse to self-advocate? How does the truth of 1 John 2:1 heal and calm that impulse? (pp. 92–93)

10. Is there some way in your heart right now that you are defending yourself, which God is calling you to lay down and to rest completely on the advocacy of Jesus Christ on your behalf? (pp. 93–94)

LESSON 5

. . . a friend of tax collectors and sinners!

MATTHEW 11:19

Chapters 10–12

Teaching Video 5

1. What is the distinct contribution Jonathan Edwards makes to how we should think about the heart of Christ? (pp. 95–96)

2. Do you think much in terms of beauty when you think of God or of Christ? (pp. 96–98)

3. Are you "romancing" the heart of Christ? What would it mean to do so? (p. 99)

4. Is Jesus a human right now? What is the implication of this for how we are to understand Christ's heart? (pp. 103–4)

5. What is the contribution B. B. Warfield makes to our understanding of the heart of Christ? (pp. 105–11)

6. What is the connection between Christ's compassion and his anger? Are these two at odds? Why or why not? (pp. 108–9)

7. What might it mean for Jesus to be angry with you? (pp. 111–12)

8. Do you find it instinctively irreverent to speak of Christ as our friend? What in your life experience informs your answer? (p. 113)

9. In what ways is Jesus Christ the perfect friend, a better friend than any human ever could be? (pp. 115–20)

10. What does it mean that Jesus is your companion? (pp. 117–18)

LESSON 6

I will ask the Father, and he will give you another Helper.

JOHN 14:16

Chapters 13 & 14

Teaching Video 6

1. What aspect of the Spirit is chapter 13 drawing out? Have you thought about this side to the Holy Spirit before? (pp. 121–22)

2. How does Thomas Goodwin explain the purpose of Christ's going away and the Spirit's coming? (pp. 123–24)

3. What are the implications of the fact that the Holy Spirit is not an impersonal force but a person? (pp. 124–25)

4. What does 1 Corinthians 2:12 teach us about the role of the Spirit? (p. 125)

5. What is chapter 13 saying about the connection between the Holy Spirit and the heart of Christ? How does this affect the way in which you go about your life of Christian discipleship? (pp. 125–26)

6. Consider the quote by A. W. Tozer that kicks off chapter 14. What first comes into your mind when you think about God? (p. 127)

7. When you think of the Father, do you tend to think of him as somehow less loving than the Son? Is this an accurate way of thinking? Why or why not? (pp. 128–29)

8. Ponder the phrase "the Father of mercies" in 2 Corinthians 1:3. Have you collapsed yet into a daily mindfulness that this is who God the Father is? If not, why? (pp. 129–30)

9. Review the quote from Goodwin on pages 131–32. What wounds in your own heart do the Father's perfect mercies need to heal?

10. How is your prayer life with the Father changed as you consider the truths of pages 132–33? How is your communion with God affected?

LESSON 7

He does not afflict from his heart.

LAMENTATIONS 3:33

Chapters 15 & 16

Teaching Video 7

1. As we turn now to the Old Testament, do you expect the vision of heaven's heart to dampen somewhat? Do you think of the Old Testament as giving us a cooler or more calculating deity? Do the opening paragraphs of chapter 15 surprise you in any way? (pp. 135–36)

2. Have you read Lamentations before? What is your sense of the mood and tone and message of the book? What do we find at the literary high point of the book? (pp. 136–37)

3. In what ways does Lamentations 3:32–33 affirm divine sovereignty (God's supreme control of everything that washes into our lives)? (pp. 137–38)

4. What does it mean that God does not afflict his people "from his heart" (Lam. 3:33)? (pp. 138–41)

5. What does it mean for your own heart and life that judgment is God's "strange" work and mercy his "natural" work? Have you thought of God like this before? (pp. 142–44)

6. What do you think of when you hear the phrase "the glory of God"? Read Exodus 33:18–19, along with 34:6–7. How does God himself apparently define his glory? How does a text such as Psalm 138:5–6 clarify the point? (pp. 145–47)

7. Have you considered before that God is said to be "provoked to anger" time after time throughout the Old Testament, but never "provoked to love" or "provoked to mercy"? What does this mean for you right now as you navigate life? (pp. 148–49)

8. What is the relationship between "keeping steadfast love for thousands" and "visiting the iniquity of the fathers . . . to the third and the fourth generation" (Ex. 34:7)? How does this comfort you? (pp. 149–50)

9. As you are reading this book, are you letting your own "natural assumption about who God is" melt away? If so, what is replacing it? (p. 151)

10. How is Exodus 34:6–7 fulfilled in the New Testament? (pp. 152–53)

LESSON 8

My heart yearns for him.

JEREMIAH 31:20

Chapters 17 & 18

Teaching Video 8

1. Have you ever said to someone, in the wake of a mysterious providence in life, "God's ways are not our ways"? What did you mean by that?

2. In light of Isaiah 55:6–9, what is the specific meaning of the Bible when it says that God's ways are not our ways? (pp. 155–57)

3. We know intuitively that God is not like us. But what do we learn from Isaiah 55 and Psalm 103 about the deepest way in which God is not like us, and what does this tell us about the way we fallen humans are hardwired? (pp. 157–58)

4. "He isn't like you. Even the most intense of human love is but the faintest echo of heaven's cascading abundance." Do you believe this? How does this affect the way you live your Christian life today? (p. 160)

5. Where are the two places God most loves to dwell, according to Isaiah 57:15? How does this connect with Matthew 11:29 and with your own life? (pp. 161–62)

6. Given the thrust of the first twenty-nine chapters of Jeremiah, what would you expect to find in chapters 30–33, as God gives his response to the first twenty-nine chapters? What do we in fact discover? (pp. 163–65)

7. What is the exact Hebrew word for "heart" as used in Jeremiah 31:20? How would you put into your own words what we are being told about who God is? (p. 165)

8. Do you think of God as yearning for you? What does this do for you as you ponder this truth? (pp. 165–67)

9. What is the point of Thomas Goodwin's statement on page 167? How would you put it into your own words?

10. Have you considered the possibility that one of the most grievous errors in your life is deflecting rather than letting in the oceanic love of God? Do you feel reluctant to let him love you? Why or why not? (pp. 168–70)

LESSON 9

But God, being rich in mercy . . .

EPHESIANS 2:4

Chapters 19–21

Teaching Video 9

1. Have you ever considered that God tells us he is "rich" in something in only one place? If he is rich in mercy more than in anything else, what does this mean for the way in which you relate to him today? (pp. 171–72)

2. What is the significance of the word *being* in the phrase "God, being rich in mercy . . ."?

3. Paul includes himself in the indictment he describes: "among whom we all once lived . . ." (Eph. 2:3). How can he, the former scrupulous Pharisee who kept all God's rules meticulously, include himself in this indictment? (pp. 176–77)

4. What is the proof of God's rich mercy in your life, despite all your hardships and sins? (pp. 178–80)

5. Do you see in yourself the subtle, chronic tendency to attempt to strengthen your standing with God based on how you are performing spiritually? (pp. 181–82)

6. What does it mean that Paul speaks of being "of works" in Galatians 3:10? Do you identify yourself with this description? (pp. 184–85)

7. How does Christ's work, and the heart from which that atoning work flowed, address your "of-works-ness"? (pp. 185–88)

8. Do you have a harder time believing God fully forgives your present sins as a Christian than believing that he forgives your past sins as a non-Christian? Why or why not? (pp. 189–90)

9. How would you put into your own words the inner logic of Romans 5:6–11? How does that logic apply to your ongoing life as a disciple of Christ? (pp. 190–94)

10. Is it possible for you who are in Christ to become any more secure in the heart of Christ than you are right now? Will you be more secure in heaven than you are now? (pp. 194–95)

LESSON 10

He loved them to the end.

JOHN 13:1

Chapters 22 & 23

Teaching Video 10

1. When you think about the love of Christ, do you find yourself believing that Christ loved you at the point of your conversion, but that his love slowly powers down as you move through life, failing him time and again? Is your thinking accurate? (pp. 197–98)

2. Put John 13:1 into your own words. What is John telling us about who Jesus is? (pp. 198–99)

3. Have you considered deeply what happened at the cross of Christ? Explain in your own words what Jesus bore on the cross. (pp. 199–202)

4. What is John Bunyan saying in the quote on pages 202–3? What does Bunyan's statement mean for your own everyday existence?

5. What will those who are not "his own" experience from Jesus Christ? But how is that fate reversed for those who are "his own"? (pp. 203–4)

6. What are some ways in which we glorify God? What is one way we glorify God, according to Jonathan Edwards? (pp. 205–6)

7. In another place Edwards sets God's "majesty and greatness" alongside his "gentleness and sweetness." What is Edwards's point? (pp. 207–8)

8. What, according to Ephesians 2:7, is the point of heaven? Is this how you think of what we will be enjoying for all eternity? (pp. 208–9)

9. Ponder what words such as "immeasurable" and "riches" and "kindness" mean in Ephesians 2:7. What are some fears or anxieties in your life right now that do not loom as large in light of these eternal realities just around the corner for those of us in Christ? (pp. 210–11)

10. What does this chapter and its reflection on Ephesians 2:7 mean for you for the rest of this year? What worries you right now, which you can be freed into entrusting to God, mindful of the eternity inevitably awaiting you? (pp. 211–13)

STUDY NOTES

STUDY NOTES

STUDY NOTES

STUDY NOTES

STUDY NOTES

STUDY NOTES

STUDY NOTES

STUDY NOTES

STUDY NOTES

STUDY NOTES